Cambridge Discovery Readers

Level 3

Series editor: Nicholas Tims

A Little Trouble in the Yorkshire Dales

Richard MacAndrew

CAMBRI[
UNIVERSITY I

CAMBRIDGE UNIVERSITY PRESS
Cambridge, New York, Melbourne, Madrid, Cape Town, Singapore, São Paulo, Delhi

Cambridge University Press
Basílica 17, 28020 Madrid, Spain

www.cambridge.org
Information on this title: www.cambridge.org/9788483235843

First published 2009
Reprinted 2009

Richard MacAndrew has asserted his right to be identified as the Author of the Work
in accordance with the Copyright, Design and Patents Act 1988.

Printed in Spain by Gráficas Varona, S.A.

ISBN 978-84-832-3584-3 paperback; legal deposit: S.932-2009
ISBN 978-84-832-3582-9 paperback with CD (audio) / CD-ROM (Windows, Mac,
Linux) pack; legal deposit: S.221-2009

No character in this work is based on any person living or dead.
Any resemblance to an actual person or situation is purely accidental.

With thanks to the people of Arkengarthdale, North Yorkshire, for their friendship,
hospitality and good humour.

Illustrations by Craig Howarth

Audio recording by BraveArts, S.L.

Exercises by Peter McDonnell

The publishers are grateful to the following for permission to reproduce
photographic material:

© ZenShui | Laurence Mouton | PhotoAlto Agency RF Collections | Getty Images
for cover image

The paper that this book has been printed on is produced using an elemental
chlorine free (ECF) process at mills registered to ISO14001 (2004), the
environmental management standard. The mills source their wood fibre from
sustainable forests. No hardwood pulp is used in the production of this paper.

Contents

People in the story

Mary Lawson: a fifteen-year-old girl; Andy Lawson's twin sister

Andy Lawson: a fifteen-year-old boy; Mary Lawson's twin brother

David Lawson: Mary and Andy Lawson's father

Gladys Whitehead: David Lawson's sister; Mary and Andy's aunt

Lord Fitch: the owner of Arkle House

Jack: works for Lord Fitch

Martin: works for Lord Fitch

David Metcalfe: a private detective

Inspector Rawlinson: a police officer

BEFORE YOU READ

 Look at *People in the story* and the pictures in the first chapter. Answer the questions.

1 Who are the main characters in this part of the story?

2 Describe where the action takes place.

Places in the story

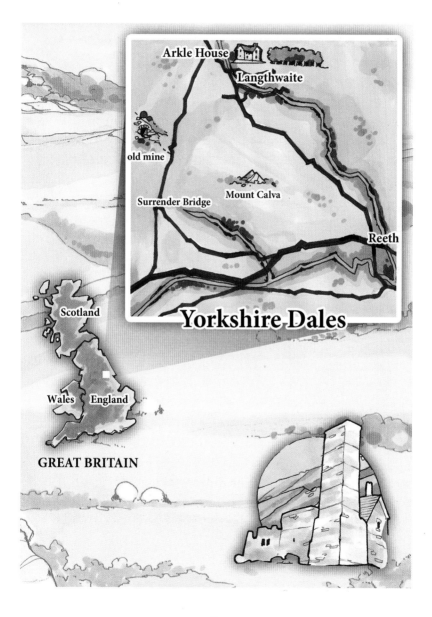

Arkle House

Langthwaite

old mine

Mount Calva

Surrender Bridge

Reeth

Scotland

Yorkshire Dales

Wales   England

GREAT BRITAIN

Chapter 1

Discovering an old mine

YORKSHIRE EVENING NEWS
Arkle House papers sold for £75,000

A suitcase full of old papers dating from the nineteenth century was sold this morning for £75,000.

The suitcase was discovered last year in a farmhouse near Reeth, North Yorkshire. Inside it were photographs, letters, bills and other papers that once belonged to Sir Francis Goodwin.

Sir Francis, the owner of Arkle House in Arkendale from 1802 to his death in 1866, was always thought to be extremely rich. However, after his death, his children and grandchildren were surprised to discover that he had left almost no money. There are many stories of undiscovered money, or even gold, hidden somewhere in the grounds of Arkle House, or possibly in the house itself. But nothing has ever been found.

The suitcase was bought by Lord[1] Fitch, the present owner of Arkle House. Thomas Goodwin, the great-great-grandson of Sir Francis, was also interested in the papers. However, he was unable to offer as much for them as Lord Fitch.

'What's that?' asked Andy, pointing to a dark area on the side of the hill in front of him and his sister.

'I've no idea,' said Mary. 'Let's go and have a look.'

Andrew, always called Andy, and Mary Lawson were on holiday in the Yorkshire Dales[2] in the north of England. The Yorkshire Dales are very beautiful: hills and dales, up and down, wild countryside on the tops of the hills, sleepy villages, rivers and farms in the dales at the bottom. Today Andy and Mary were out cycling in the hills.

'Let's leave our bikes here,' said Andy, putting his bike against a large stone.

'Good thinking,' said Mary, placing her bike carefully on the ground. 'There's no one around to steal them.'

They hadn't seen anyone at all for the last hour. The countryside was completely empty of people: no other mountain bikers, no walkers – just birds, lots of rabbits and a few sheep.

There was a kind of road going up the side of the hill. Together Andy and Mary climbed until they were standing in front of a large hole in the side of the hill.

'It's very dark in there,' said Andy. 'What do you think it is?'

'It's a mine,' said Mary, sounding very sure of herself. 'You know, where people dig³ into the ground looking for a metal like gold or silver or something like that.'

'You mean there's gold here in the dales?' said Andy, looking rather surprised.

'No, silly,' said Mary. 'Dad was telling me about it last night. There are lots of mines in this part of the dales, but they're lead mines. And if you ever listened in your geography class, you'd know that lead is a metal that's used on roofs.'

'Yeah, yeah,' said Andy. 'So why aren't they still digging for it now, Miss Clever?'

'Because they've taken out almost all the lead that is there,' said Mary, and she started to take off her backpack and look inside it.

'What are you looking for?' asked Andy.

'My torch,' replied Mary. 'I know it's here somewhere and we're going to need some light if we want to go and have a look inside.'

'But ...' Andy looked into the entrance to the mine and shook his head a little. 'Why? It's dark and cold and wet and probably dangerous.'

'Here it is,' said Mary, finally pulling a torch out of her backpack and turning it on and off quickly to check that it worked.

'Let's go,' she said and started to walk into the mine, holding the torch in front of her.

Andy shook his head again and followed her in. He and Mary were the same age, fifteen – they were twins – but everything else about them was different. He was 180 centimetres tall; she was shorter. He had short red hair; she had long brown hair. He had blue eyes; she had brown eyes. And if they got into trouble, it was usually her fault. He didn't really want to go into the mine, but he thought he should go with her to make sure she was OK.

'I thought mines went downwards into the ground,' he said, as they moved carefully along.

'Some do,' said Mary. 'And some go flat, straight into the side of a hill.'

The floor of the mine was even and the roof was low. Both Mary and Andy had to be careful not to hit their heads. In one or two places someone had put pieces of wood across the roof of the mine to stop it falling down. When they came to one of these places, Mary shone the torch on the wood.

'Look at that,' she said.

'What?'

'Well, those are new pieces of wood,' she said. 'Someone's been looking after this mine.'

'Maybe they're still looking for lead,' said Andy.

Mary did not reply. She just kept moving forward into the mine, waving her torch slowly from side to side. Then suddenly she stopped.

Andy came up beside her. The torch was lighting up a new wooden door in the side wall. There was a lock on the door. Mary went over and pulled at the lock, but it didn't open. She pulled at the door, but that didn't open either.

'I think you should leave it now,' said Andy.

'Why?' asked Mary.

'Well, if you get it open, someone's going to know we've been here,' he replied. 'And they might not like that.'

'Why not?' asked Mary.

'There's a lock on the door, stupid,' said Andy. 'That probably means they don't want people to go in there.'

He put a hand on his sister's arm.

'Come on,' he said. 'I really think we should go. If someone finds us here, we could be in trouble.'

Mary said nothing for a moment, then she spoke, 'OK, Mr Careful. You're right, as usual. Let's go.'

A few minutes later they were back out in the warm afternoon sunshine. They jogged back down the hill and picked up their bikes.

Before getting on his bike, Andy looked round at the hills. This place is beautiful, he thought, not for the first time. But what was that? Up on the side of one of the other hills the sunlight had caught something. A mirror? It couldn't be. Then the light disappeared and Andy saw a head move. Someone was watching them! Through binoculars![4] A man in a dark blue jacket.

'Look. There's someone watching us,' said Andy. 'Up on the side of the hill over there.'

11

Mary looked up, but by then the man had gone.

'Too late,' said Andy. 'He's gone. Come on. Let's get going.'

Quickly, they started cycling back the way they had come. A few minutes later, as they came over the top of a hill and started down the other side, they saw a Land Rover driving towards them along the dirt road. The Land Rover stopped and a man got out, waiting for them to reach him. He was youngish, maybe twenty-five to thirty years old, and dressed in a green and brown shirt and trousers, and walking boots. He had dark hair, very light blue eyes and an unfriendly look.

Andy and Mary had to stop and get off their bikes to get past the Land Rover.

'Where have you been?' asked the man, as they walked up to him. 'Down any of the mines?'

LOOKING BACK

 Check your answers to *Before you read* on page 4.

ACTIVITIES

2 Complete the sentences with the names in the box.

> ~~Sir Francis Goodwin~~   Andy   Thomas Goodwin
> Andy and Mary's dad   Lord Fitch   Andy and Mary

1 *Sir Francis Goodwin* died a long time ago.
2 .... lives in Arkle House.
3 .... wanted to buy Sir Francis's papers.
4 .... find a mine.
5 .... told Mary about the mines in Yorkshire.
6 .... doesn't want to go into the mine.

3 Underline the correct words in each sentence.
1 They found Sir Francis's papers in *Arkle House / a farmhouse*.
2 Andy and Mary are in *a big city / the countryside*.
3 Andy and Mary are *cycling / walking* in the dales.
4 In the past, there was *more / less* lead in the Yorkshire Dales than there is now.
5 Andy *is / isn't* older than Mary.
6 The twins find a *door / torch* in the mine.

4 Match the two parts of the sentences.
  1 Thomas Goodwin wanted to buy Sir Francis's papers but ☐ c
  2 Mary looks for her torch because ☐
  3 Andy doesn't want to go into the mine, but ☐
  4 Mary and Andy know that people still use the mine because ☐
  5 A man is watching Andy and Mary, but ☐
  6 The man in the Land Rover stops because ☐

  a he follows Mary into it.
  b Mary doesn't see him.
  c Lord Fitch could pay more than him.
  d there are new pieces of wood on the roof.
  e he wants to talk to Andy and Mary.
  f it's very dark in the mine.

5 Answer the questions.
  1 Why are Andy and Mary in the Yorkshire Dales?
     Because they're on holiday.
  2 Why doesn't Andy want to go into the mine?

  3 How does Andy know that someone is watching him?

  4 What does the man ask the twins?

LOOKING FORWARD

6 Tick (✓) what you think happens in the next two chapters.
  1 Andy and Mary see the man with the binoculars again. ☐
  2 Andy and Mary go back to the mine. ☐

15

Chapter 2

The missing money

Mary immediately felt that 'yes' was not the right answer.

'What mines?' she asked.

'Mines,' said the man. 'Lead mines. Holes in the ground. Holes in the side of the hills. Have you been in any?'

'No,' said Andy, realising what Mary was doing. 'We haven't seen any, actually.'

'Good,' said the man. 'Well, if you do see any, keep out. They're dangerous. Nobody's looked after them for the last hundred years. The roof could fall in. You could fall down a hole you don't see. Keep out of them.'

'Right,' said Mary. 'We will.'

The man turned and got back into the Land Rover. Mary and Andy pulled their bikes to the side of the road so that the man could drive past. When he had left over the top of the hill, the teenagers looked at each other. They both realised it had been a good idea not to tell the man where they had been. Sometimes they didn't need to speak. They just knew what the other one was thinking – perhaps it was because they were twins.

'Right,' said Mary. 'Let's get back.'

Andy started off with Mary following behind, but soon she rode up beside Andy and cycled next to him.

'I've been thinking,' she said.

'Oh no,' thought Andy, but he didn't say anything. It was usually Mary's ideas that got them into trouble.

'That man said that no one looked after the mines any more. In fact no one has looked after the mines for over a hundred years,' continued Mary. 'But someone has been looking after the one we went into.'

'True,' said Andy.

'And that man didn't seem very friendly at all,' said Mary. 'But most people here are extremely friendly.'

Andy didn't say anything.

'That's quite surprising,' Mary went on.

'Not everyone is friendly all the time,' said Andy.

They cycled a little further.

'I'd like to know what's behind that door,' said Mary.

'No,' said Andy quickly.

'No what?'

Andy stopped his bike and Mary stopped too. Andy looked at her very seriously.

'No, we're not going to try and see what's behind that door,' he said.

'I didn't mean—' began Mary.

'Yes, you did,' said Andy. 'You were thinking it would be a good idea to go back. Well, it's not a good idea. That man didn't look very friendly and I'd be quite happy not to meet him again. No, no, no. We're not going back.'

Andy started cycling again and Mary followed him.

Ten minutes later they cycled down the hill and entered the village of Langthwaite. It was very small: a few houses, a church and a pub, no shop, no post office, no bank. They stopped in front of the house where they were staying.

Sitting outside in the sun was their Aunt Gladys. Gladys was their father's older sister and she had lived in Arkendale since she got married. She was about 160 centimetres tall with short brown hair, and she was wearing a blue and white shirt and jeans. Her husband had died a few years before, but she had stayed in Arkendale because that's where all her friends were. Andy and Mary and their father, David, were staying with Gladys for a couple of weeks. For Andy and Mary it was a holiday; for David Lawson, their father, it was work. He was an architect and he was doing some work at Arkle House, a very big house further up the dale. Their mother, Ellen, was joining them next week.

'Hello, you two,' said Aunt Gladys. 'Have you had a good afternoon?'

'Yes,' said Mary. 'We've been cycling up in the hills by Surrender Bridge. And we—'

'And we're really hungry,' said Andy quickly – so that Mary had to stop talking. 'Are we having one of your famous Yorkshire teas, Aunt Gladys?'

Aunt Gladys's 'famous Yorkshire teas' meant more than just a cup of tea and a biscuit; there could be sandwiches or salads, sometimes some scones⁵ with jam and thick cream to put on them, maybe a fruitcake or a chocolate cake, biscuits, and tea, or on a hot day homemade lemonade.

'Yes, we are,' laughed Gladys. 'Go on, go inside and get washed. Your dad will be home in a few minutes.'

As Andy and Mary ran into the house, Mary said to him, 'I wasn't starting to tell Aunt Gladys about going into the mine, you know. I'm not stupid.'

Andy just looked at his sister, a small smile on his face.

'The man in the Land Rover said the mines were dangerous,' said Mary. 'I don't think Aunt Gladys is going to be too happy if she knows we've been in one. Is she?'

'Just making sure,' said Andy.

Mary just stuck her tongue out at her brother and then went to the bathroom.

Half an hour later everyone was sitting at the table in Aunt Gladys's kitchen. There were cold meats and different types of salad on the table, as well as bread and butter, a large fruitcake and a pot of tea. Andy and Mary had a tall glass of lemonade each.

'You know the old story about Sir Francis Goodwin's missing money,' said David Lawson. 'You know – everyone thought he was rich, but when he died no one found any money.'

'Because he hid it somewhere,' added Mary. 'Everyone in Arkendale knows that story. It's just that nobody knows where the money is.'

'Well, Lord Fitch thinks he's actually found the money,' said David. 'Well, gold actually.'

'What!' said Gladys. 'That's amazing!'

'Was it in a lead mine?' asked Mary.

'Yes, I think it was.' Mary's father looked at her strangely. 'How did you know that?'

'I didn't,' said Mary, 'I just—' as she felt Andy kick her under the table. 'It doesn't matter.'

'Anyway,' David continued, 'Lord Fitch told me a bit about it this morning. He was talking to some journalists about it this afternoon, so it'll probably be all over the papers tomorrow morning.'

'How did they find it?' asked Mary.

'Well, it was completely by accident. Lord Fitch is thinking of repairing one of the mines and opening it for tourists,' replied her father. 'He'd sent some of his workers into it to have a look. And they found the gold.'

'How much was there?' asked Mary.

'What's he going to do with it?' asked Andy.

'I don't know. I don't know,' laughed David Lawson. 'I was working. I didn't have much time to chat. But we're all invited up to Arkle House tomorrow afternoon, so you can ask him these questions yourselves, if you want to. Though I did tell him I thought you'd be out cycling or something and probably wouldn't want to come.'

'No, no,' said Mary. 'We want to come. Don't we, Andy?' Mary looked her brother straight in the eyes and opened her eyes wide.

Andy realised his sister really wanted to meet Lord Fitch. So did he, actually. He looked at his father.

David Lawson was in his early forties and about 190 centimetres tall. He was wearing a light blue shirt and grey trousers, and had red hair like his son. He was looking a bit surprised – probably because these days Mary preferred to spend time with people her own age rather than adults.

'I've never met a lord before,' said Andy. 'I think it might be interesting. And I'd like to hear about the gold.' He laughed. 'Perhaps if we become friends with him, he'll give us some.'

Everyone laughed.

Then Mary said, 'Maybe he'll take us into the mine and show us where he found it.'

David Lawson looked seriously at Mary and waved a finger at her.

'I know you, Mary Lawson,' he said. 'Don't you even think of going into a lead mine! With or without Lord Fitch. I'm sure there is no more gold to find and lead mines are very dangerous places. OK?'

'OK, Dad,' said Mary. But, as she spoke, she was thinking, 'Why do adults always try and stop me having fun? If I want to find out what's behind the door we found in the mine, I will. And now I think I do want to find out.'

She looked at Andy again and felt him kick her again under the table. For the second time that evening she stuck her tongue out at him.

'Stop it, you two!' said their father.

Chapter 3

At Reeth Show

The next day was the day of Reeth Show. The village of Reeth was in Swaledale, the next dale to Arkendale, and it was the nearest village with any shops. Every year at this time of year there was a show in a field just outside Reeth. At this show there were all sorts of competitions: competitions to see who had grown the biggest vegetables, who could make the best cakes, who could take the best photographs; competitions to see which farmer had the best sheep and which had the cleverest sheepdog. There was a running race to the top of the nearest hill and back. There were tents where people sold things: clothes, boots, shoes, flowers, photographs of the dales, Yorkshire cheeses, cakes, Swaledale honey, hot dogs, ice creams, all sorts of things. Everyone in Swaledale and Arkendale would be at the show at some time during the day.

In the morning David Lawson went to work at Arkle House and Gladys took Andy and Mary to the show.

'You two go and have a look round,' Gladys told the teenagers as they got out of her car. 'I'm going to see if my fruitcake has won a prize. I'll meet you back at the car in an hour.'

Andy and Mary walked slowly round the show ground. They watched a sheepdog bring six sheep down a field and through a gate.[6] Mary bought an ice cream and then she and Andy went into the art tent, where there were lots of pictures of the dales. They looked at some of the pictures, and were just leaving when Mary put a hand on Andy's arm and pulled him back into the tent.

'Look at this painting and don't turn round,' she whispered. 'That's him. The man from the Land Rover yesterday. He's just outside the tent.'

Andy looked out of the corner of his eye. The man was less than a metre away but looking the other way. Just then another man came up to him.

'All right, Jack?'

'Yes thanks, Martin.' Land Rover man was Jack; his friend was Martin. Martin was not as tall as Jack and a bit older, with dark brown hair.

Martin stood beside Jack and they both looked out across the field away from the tent.

'Everything ready for tomorrow?' asked Martin.

Jack put his head close to Martin's.

'Keep your voice down,' Mary heard him say. She came round the other side of Andy so that she was closer than him to the two men. She put her left hand on Andy's shoulder and looked hard at the painting in front of them.

'If they turn round, they'll think we're studying the painting,' she thought. But really she was listening as hard as she could. Even then she only heard little bits of the conversation.

'read about it in the papers … the big house … moving the boxes … much more than that … the old mine … Surrender Bridge … five o'clock tomorrow morning … I'll keep it quiet'

Then Mary realised, from the way the men were speaking, that the conversation was coming to an end. She put her head close to Andy's again.

'Further back in the tent. Quick,' she whispered, and they moved back inside the tent away from the men. Mary told Andy what she had heard, but he wasn't that interested.

'I'm sure it was to do with the gold and that door we saw,' said Mary.

'You don't know that for sure,' replied Andy. 'You're probably putting two and two together and making five. You usually do. You're not very good at Maths.'

Mary stuck her tongue out at him, but she wasn't angry. She often stuck her tongue out at her brother when she didn't agree with him.

When Andy and Mary came out of the tent a few minutes later, the men had gone. There was now a large circle in the middle of the field, with people sitting all along the outside of the circle. Inside the circle some young children were riding on ponies, showing how good they were at riding.

Andy and Mary stood and watched for a few minutes. Then Andy started to look at the people watching from the other side of the circle. There were all sorts of people: farmers, tourists, old, young. As he looked along the line of faces, Andy realised that one face was looking back at him and not watching the children and their ponies. It was a man with grey hair, a grey beard and a rather red face. Clearly, the man seemed to know Andy. Andy looked away and then looked back. The man was wearing a blue jacket and had some binoculars round his neck.

'The man on the hill from yesterday,' thought Andy. 'The one who was watching us.'

The man looked hard at Andy and then started to walk along the outside of the circle towards him.

'Let's go,' said Andy, taking Mary by the hand and pulling her along.

'What? Why? Where are we going?' she asked, surprised.

'There's a man over there. I'm sure he was the one watching us yesterday up by the mine. He probably saw us come out of it. And now he's coming over, as if he wants to talk to us.'

Andy looked behind him. The crowd was quite large, so it would take the man a minute to get through to them.

'Come on,' said Mary. 'Let's run. Back to the car.'

They were about fifty metres from the car when Gladys appeared out of a tent, with a bag of homemade biscuits in one hand.

'Have you had enough already?' she asked.

'Yes,' said Andy. 'We're getting a bit bored.'

'Well, OK then,' said Gladys.

'I'll race you to the car,' said Andy to Mary, and they both ran towards Gladys's car. Gladys laughed and followed them more slowly.

Two minutes later Andy turned and looked out of the back window of the car as they drove away. The man with grey hair was standing in the car park, watching them.

'That was lucky,' thought Andy. 'But who is he? And what does he want? Arkendale is a small place. We'll have to talk to him sooner or later.'

And he was right.

LOOKING BACK

● ●

1 Check your answer to *Looking forward* on page 15.

ACTIVITIES

● ●

2 Are the sentences true (*T*) or false (*F*)?

1 The Lawsons are staying in a hotel. ☐F☐
2 David Lawson is on holiday in the Yorkshire Dales. ☐
3 David's wife, Ellen, isn't in the Yorkshire Dales. ☐
4 Mary and Andy don't tell their aunt about the mine. ☐
5 Lord Fitch told David some news about Sir Francis Goodwin's money. ☐
6 Lord Fitch's workers were looking for gold in the mine. ☐
7 The twins want to meet Lord Fitch. ☐
8 Mary doesn't plan to do what her father tells her to do. ☐

3 Put the sentences in order.

At Reeth Show Andy and Mary ...

1 see the man with the binoculars. ☐
2 start running back to the car. ☐
3 look at some pictures. ☐
4 watch some children riding ponies. ☐
5 watch a sheepdog. ☐1☐
6 listen to a conversation. ☐
7 leave the art tent. ☐
8 meet their aunt. ☐

4 <u>Underline</u> the correct words in each sentence.

1 The man says that the mines are *new / not safe / his*.

2 Andy *wants / doesn't want / isn't sure if he wants* to go back to the mine.

3 Gladys is *Ellen's sister / David's sister / David's friend*.

4 Mary and Andy go to Reeth Show with their *father / aunt / friend Martin*.

5 In the art tent, the twins *talk to / argue with / listen to* the Land Rover man.

6 The Land Rover man and Martin make plans for the next *week / morning / month*.

7 Mary and Andy *run away from / talk to / stick their tongue out at* the man with the binoculars.

5 Answer the questions.

1 Why is Mary surprised that the man with the Land Rover was unfriendly?

....

2 Why don't the children tell their aunt about going into the mine?

....

3 Why doesn't Gladys stay with the children at Reeth Show?

....

4 What does Mary think Martin and Jack's conversation is about?

....

LOOKING FORWARD

• •

6 What do you think? Answer the questions.

1 Will Andy and Mary decide to go back to the mine?

....

2 Will they talk to the man with the binoculars?

....

Chapter 4

Meeting Lord Fitch

'How nice to meet you!' said Lord Fitch, shaking hands first with Mary and then with Andy. 'I've heard a lot about you from your father. Are you enjoying your time in Arkendale?'

Andy and Mary and David Lawson were in the large sitting room at Arkle House with Lord Fitch. They all sat down. There were tea and biscuits on the table in front of them. Gladys had decided not to come. She had to take her neighbour, an old woman of ninety-three, to the dentist in Richmond.

'It's great,' said Andy.

'We're having a fantastic time,' said Mary.

'They just love being free to cycle off into the countryside and spend all day by themselves,' said David Lawson to Lord Fitch.

'That's the best bit about it,' said Andy with a smile on his face, 'being able to get away from our parents!'

Lord Fitch and David Lawson laughed.

Lord Fitch was a tall man. He was dressed in country browns: dark brown trousers, light brown shirt, dark brown tie, and, even though it was a warm day, a greeny brown jacket. He had fair hair and a thin fair moustache.

'Can I ask you about the gold?' said Mary, sitting forward on the sofa.

'Of course,' said Lord Fitch, looking across the room at Mary.

'Is it really Sir Francis Goodwin's gold?'

'It certainly looks like it,' answered Lord Fitch. 'There are numbers and letters on it which show that it was made at the beginning of the nineteenth century.'

'And how much gold is there?' asked Mary.

'About ten kilos.'

'Is that worth a lot of money?' asked Andy.

'Gold costs about £14,000 a kilo at the moment so, yes, about £140,000,' replied Lord Fitch.

'What are you going to do with it?' asked Andy.

Lord Fitch smiled.

'Well, first I had to decide if it belonged to me or not,' he said. 'I mean, although it was found on my land, it wasn't really my gold.'

He took a drink of tea from the cup on the table in front of him and continued, 'In July last year I bought a case full of papers that once belonged to Sir Francis. His great-great-grandchildren were also interested in the papers, but I made sure I got them.'

'Why?' asked Mary.

'Well, with your father's help, I am trying to return Arkle House to what it used to be like. When the last owners were here, it was a hotel. They made a lot of changes to the building – not all of them good. Among the papers I bought were some old photographs and a lot of interesting information about the house. Because of that information, we'll be able to change the rooms back to the way they were.'

Lord Fitch stood up, walked across the room and opened one of the windows a little.

Turning back to face the room, he said, 'Sir Francis's great-great-grandchildren were rather unhappy when I bought the papers. But I felt that the papers were about the house and so they belonged here. However, I feel that the gold rightfully belongs to Sir Francis's family.'

No one spoke for a moment.

'That's very generous of you,' said David Lawson.

'I'm a generous man,' said Lord Fitch and laughed. 'No, to be honest,' he continued, 'I thought it was only fair. I mean, I have a lot of money of my own and the Goodwin family has been looking for that money for over a hundred years.'

'Where did you find the gold?' asked Mary.

Lord Fitch walked over to a large map on the wall.

'I'll show you,' he said. 'Come and have a look.'

David, Andy and Mary got up and walked over to the map.

'Here's Reeth and here's Langthwaite and Arkle House,' said Lord Fitch, showing them on the map. 'And this is where we found the gold.'

His finger was resting on a place a little further up the dale behind Arkle House, called the Windegg Lead Mine.

'How much of the land round here belongs to Arkle House?' asked Mary.

'From just behind the Windegg Mine across the dale to Surrender Bridge. And, the other way, from just outside Reeth almost to the village of Whaw,' answered Lord Fitch.

Mary looked closely at the map. The mine she and Andy had been in the day before was near Surrender Bridge, and that was on Lord Fitch's land too.

'Interesting,' thought Mary, 'that mine's a long way from the Windegg Mine.'

Half an hour later the three Lawsons were walking down the road from Arkle House back towards the village of Langthwaite and Gladys's house. A Land Rover was coming towards them and they moved off the road to let it pass. Mary looked at the driver as it passed: black hair, unfriendly face.

'Who was driving that Land Rover?' she asked her father, as they stepped back onto the road.

'One of Lord Fitch's workers, I think,' answered David Lawson. 'I've seen him around a few times. I think his name's Jack. Why?'

'Oh, nothing,' replied Mary. 'It's just that I saw him at Reeth Show this morning.'

Mary fell quiet, deep in thought, until she felt Andy touch her. She looked at him. Their father was walking a few steps ahead.

'Over to the left,' said Andy quietly, 'up the hill. The man from the show this morning. He's watching us through binoculars again.'

Mary looked up to the left and saw the man with grey hair watching them.

'He's too far away to do anything,' said Mary. 'And he probably won't come and talk to us if we're with Dad.'

'But, if he does, and he saw us come out of the mine, we could be in trouble.'

'Don't worry about it,' said Mary, sounding more sure than she felt.

'Anyway,' she continued, 'I'm still thinking about the door we found and Lord Fitch's gold.'

'What is there to think about?' asked Andy.

'Who found the gold?' asked Mary.

'Some of Lord Fitch's workers,' replied Andy.

'How does Lord Fitch know how much gold there was?' asked Mary.

'His workers probably told him.'

'What if they didn't tell him about all of it?' asked Mary.

'Why on earth[7] would you think that?' asked Andy.

'I'll tell you later.'

35

Chapter 5

An evening conversation

Later that day they sat round Gladys's kitchen table having tea. Gladys had come back from Richmond and was passing plates round to everyone.

'Has anyone seen a stranger in the dale?' she asked. 'A number of people are asking about him. A man with grey hair, a grey beard and a red face?'

Mary and Andy looked at each other. Gladys saw the look.

'Well?' she asked.

'Yes,' said Andy carefully, 'we've seen him. Why? Who is he?'

'Nobody knows,' said Gladys. 'He's been around for a week or two now, but he doesn't seem to be a tourist – not a normal tourist, anyway. And he's been spending a lot of time in Arkendale.'

Gladys passed round a bowl of salad.

'Some people think he might be a policeman of some kind and that he's checking up on the farmers.'

Mary gave Andy a look that said 'Don't talk about lead mines' and then spoke, 'He was at the show this morning.'

'And we saw him again this afternoon,' said Andy. 'When we were walking back from Arkle House, he was up on the side of the hill, watching us through binoculars.'

'Watching you?' asked David.

'I don't know if he was watching us,' replied Andy, 'but he was looking through binoculars. He was probably watching Mary. I mean, she is a bit strange.'

Mary kicked her brother under the table.

'Ouch!' said Andy.

'That's enough,' said David Lawson.

'Well,' said Gladys, picking up her knife and fork, 'if you hear anything about him, or find out anything, let me know. The farmers round here would like to know what he's doing.'

Later that evening Andy and Mary went out for a walk. There's a small river that runs along Arkendale and through Langthwaite. It's called Arkle Beck. In Langthwaite there is a bridge over the river. Andy and Mary stopped on the bridge and dropped a few stones into the water.

'OK,' said Andy. 'Tell me. What mad ideas are racing round that crazy brain[8] of yours, sister?'

Mary turned and hit Andy's arm quite hard.

'I'm not crazy,' she said.

'Ouch!' said Andy for the second time that evening, holding his arm. 'Don't do that. I didn't say you were crazy, just that you had a crazy brain.'

Mary turned back to look at the water and dropped another stone.

'I told you this afternoon,' she said, 'I don't think Lord Fitch knows everything.'

'But why do you think that?' asked Andy.

Mary turned round and rested her back against the bridge. She looked at her brother.

'Those men were talking about something secret,' she explained. 'They didn't want other people to hear. They were talking about "papers" or something being "in the papers". I can't remember which. And it was to do with "boxes". All those things could mean the gold. The news of the gold was in the papers and the gold would be in boxes.'

'Well, I understand you so far,' said Andy.

'When we saw Lord Fitch,' continued Mary, 'he told us that they found the gold up at Windegg. But the man at the show, Jack, he was talking about Surrender Bridge. That's where we saw him yesterday.'

'So?'

'So,' said Mary, 'perhaps Jack found the gold, took most of it away and hid it in the mine near Surrender Bridge. And then he just took ten kilos to Lord Fitch and said "Look what I found." How about that?'

'Possible,' said Andy. 'But there's no way you can find out for sure. Not without opening the door in the mine and we've decided that's too dangerous.'

Actually they hadn't decided that. Andy had. But he thought he'd let Mary know how he felt.

'In fact, I have thought of a way we can find out,' said Mary.

'Oh no,' thought Andy. 'Here we go – mad ideas in a crazy brain!' But he didn't say anything. He just looked at Mary and waited.

'When I was listening to them,' she began, 'I heard Jack say something about moving boxes.'

'Yes?' Andy sounded unsure.

Mary continued, 'I also heard him say something about five o'clock in the morning and the old mine at Surrender Bridge. I'm sure that's the one we found.'

'You're not thinking of—' began Andy.

'Yes,' said Mary excitedly. 'If we get up about four o'clock, we could be up at the mine a long time before they arrive. We could watch what they do. And if they have hidden some gold from Lord Fitch, then we can tell him.'

'You're joking,' said Andy. 'Four o'clock in the morning is far too early to get up. And we'd decided not to go into the mine again.'

'We don't actually have to go into the mine,' said Mary. 'We just have to hide and watch. Come on, Andy! Even if I'm wrong and there's no one there, it'll still be fun. It'll be an adventure.'

'What about Dad and Aunt Gladys?' asked Andy.

'We'll just leave a note on the kitchen table. If we're quiet, they won't hear us go. And we'll probably be back before they get up.'

*　*　*

In summer it gets light very early in the Yorkshire Dales. When Mary's clock woke her up at four o'clock in the morning, it was already light outside. She had put her clock under her pillow so it didn't wake up everyone in the house.

She got out of bed and got dressed: jeans, brown T-shirt, light brown sweatshirt. It would be cold outside at that time of the morning. Then she went quietly along to Andy's room and woke him up.

'Come on, sleepyhead,' she whispered. 'It's four o'clock. We need to be going.'

Andy quickly put on some jeans and a dark green sweatshirt. At the same time he was thinking that this was, as usual, not one of Mary's best ideas.

Quietly, the two of them went downstairs. Mary wrote a note, saying where they were going and when they would be back. She didn't put what time they were leaving. Andy unlocked the back door and they went out into the cool morning air.

Quickly, they got their bikes out of Aunt Gladys's garage and started up the hill towards Surrender Bridge. Andy had a bad feeling about this plan of Mary's, but at four o'clock in the morning he was too tired to argue with her.

LOOKING BACK

1 Check your answers to *Looking forward* on page 29.

ACTIVITIES

2 <u>Underline</u> the correct words in each sentence.

1 *Gladys* / <u>*David*</u> told Lord Fitch about Andy and Mary.
2 The price of gold is *£14,000* / *£140,000* per kilo.
3 Lord Fitch wants to make Arkle House *into a hotel* / *how it was before*.
4 Lord Fitch is going to give the gold to *David's* / *Sir Francis's* family.
5 They found the gold at *Surrender* / *Windegg* Mine.
6 The man in the Land Rover works for *the police* / *Lord Fitch*.

3 Complete the sentences with the words in the box.

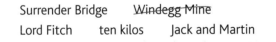

Surrender Bridge ~~Windegg Mine~~
Lord Fitch   ten kilos   Jack and Martin

1 Mary thinks that Jack found a lot of gold at ..... *Windegg Mine* .....
2 Jack took most of the gold to a mine near ....
3 Jack left only .... of the gold in Windegg Mine.
4 Jack then told .... about the ten kilos of gold in Windegg Mine.
5 Mary wants to watch what .... do at the mine.

42

4 What do the underlined words refer to in these lines from the text?

1 'That's the best bit about <u>it</u>' (page 30) 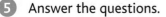 *the holiday*

2 'but I made sure I got <u>them</u>.' (page 32) ....

3 Mary looked at the driver as <u>it</u> passed. (page 34)

....

4 'That's where we saw <u>him</u> yesterday.' (page 39)

....

5 'I'm sure that's <u>the one</u> we found.' (page 39)

....

6 Quietly, the two of <u>them</u> went downstairs. (page 40)

....

5 Answer the questions.

1 What does Lord Fitch look like?

....

2 Who does Andy see watching him and Mary at the end of Chapter 4?

....

3 Who does Aunt Gladys ask the twins about when they're having tea?

....

4 Where are Mary and Andy going at the end of Chapter 5?

....

LOOKING FORWARD
● ●

6 Tick (✓) what you think happens in the next two chapters.

1 Gladys goes to Surrender Bridge. ☐
2 Jack and Martin are at Surrender Bridge. ☐

Chapter 6

An early morning adventure

It took half an hour for Andy and Mary to reach Surrender Bridge. Once there they started up the dirt road towards the mine. There seemed to be hundreds of rabbits running through the grass and over the stones beside the road.

Ten minutes later they stopped at the bottom of the road that led up to the entrance to the mine.

'We can't leave our bikes here,' said Mary as they stopped. She looked round for a good hiding place.

'How about up there?' she said. There was a hill opposite the mine entrance with a dry stone wall[9] running along the side of it.

'We could go behind the wall,' said Andy. 'We won't be too near the mine. But we'll be able to see everything that goes on both down here and up at the entrance to the mine.'

'Good idea,' said Mary.

The teenagers pushed their bikes up the hill and laid them on the ground behind the wall. Then they sat down to wait to see if Jack arrived.

Some time later Andy looked at his watch.

'It's ten past five,' he said. 'Maybe they're not coming.'

'Give them another ten minutes,' said Mary.

But only a couple more minutes had passed, before the early morning quiet was broken by the sound of two Land Rover engines.

Andy and Mary watched them arrive. Mary lay on her stomach and looked round the end of the wall; Andy stood up and looked over the top of it, keeping his head as low as possible.

44

One of the Land Rovers drove up the hill to the entrance to the mine. It turned round and drove backwards up to the entrance. The other one stopped at the bottom. The driver's door opened and Jack got out. He opened the back door and a brown and white dog jumped out and ran into the long grass. Jack started walking up the hill.

Jack called to the dog, and it ran after him.

Martin got out of the Land Rover by the entrance to the mine. He opened the back door and left it open. Then he went into the mine. Jack reached the mine entrance and went in too. His dog, Poppy, looked into the mine but stayed outside. Then she ran away again into the long grass around the mine, nose to the ground.

After a few minutes Martin and Jack came out of the mine, carrying a long box. It was made of wood and looked old and very heavy. They put it into the back of the Land Rover and then went back into the mine. Soon they came out with another box. They put that in the Land Rover too.

Over the next twenty minutes, the two men brought out ten boxes of different sizes, putting all of them in the Land Rover until there was very little room left. Then Martin drove the Land Rover down to the bottom of the hill next to the second Land Rover.

'We've got to see what's in those boxes,' whispered Mary.

'We can't,' replied Andy. 'We can't get down there without them seeing us.'

Martin got out of his Land Rover and started to walk towards the other one. Jack stood by the entrance to the mine and watched him.

Then suddenly there was a noise in the grass near Mary and Andy. A bird flew up into the air near them, with Poppy, the dog, racing after it. The bird flew up and away, but Poppy saw Mary and Andy. Surprised, she stopped and then started to bark at them.

'Woof! Woof!' she went.

'Shh!' Mary tried to make the dog be quiet, but it was no good. The dog took a few steps back but continued to make even more noise.

'Woof! Woof! Woof! Woof!'

Both men looked up and across to where the dog was. Martin turned and looked up at Jack.

'Come on, Jack! Let's go and see what she's found,' he said, and started climbing the hill towards the teenagers. Jack ran down from the mine and started climbing up the hill too.

Poppy continued to bark at Andy and Mary, and Mary took a quick look round the end of the wall to see what the men were doing.

'Oh no!' she said when she saw the men coming up the hill towards them. 'Quick, Andy, we've got to get out of here.'

She and Andy both picked up their bikes and started to push them around the end of the wall, but they were too slow. Poppy was barking and jumping backwards and forwards in front of them. It was impossible to pass her to get on the bikes. And then it was too late.

Martin arrived first. He took Mary by the arm and pulled her away from her bike. It fell to the ground.

'Let go!' she shouted. 'Let me go!'

She tried to fight and kick Martin to get away, but he took hold of both her arms and pushed her face forwards against the dry stone wall. Mary realised she was caught and stopped fighting.

Andy dropped his bike and started to run, but by then Jack had reached the wall. Andy was quick, but no match for Jack. Within ten metres Jack had reached him. He jumped on Andy's back and they both fell to the ground. Within moments he had taken Andy's right hand and pushed it up behind his shoulders.

'Stop!' shouted Andy. 'You're hurting me.'

Jack stood up, pulling Andy to his feet as well, but keeping Andy's hand up behind his back.

He looked across at Mary and then at the back of Andy's head in front of him.

'Those kids!' he said angrily. 'That's all we need.'

'What are we going to do with them, Jack?' asked Martin.

'A little accident, I think,' answered Jack. 'These mines are dangerous places. And these kids should know. I told them so myself only a couple of days ago.'

Chapter 7

The mines are dangerous

Five minutes later Jack and Martin were pushing the teenagers into the mine. They had put their bikes into the back of the empty Land Rover.

'We don't want anyone to find those bikes near here,' Jack had said. 'We'll leave them near a different mine.'

Martin had a torch and was lighting up the way ahead. Soon they reached the door with the lock that the teenagers had found two days before. The door was now open. There was a lamp inside giving off a little light and showing what seemed to be a long room, maybe even a tunnel.[10] There were six boxes still left. The top of one of the boxes was broken and, in the half light, Mary could see the shine of gold.

'I was right,' said Mary. 'You *are* stealing the gold.'

'Shut up!' said Jack angrily. 'This is nothing to do with you.'

He looked at Martin.

'Get those last boxes out of here,' he ordered. 'We need to get back in time to meet the helicopter.'

Quickly, Martin pulled the boxes along the ground and out through the door.

Jack pushed both the teenagers in through the door.

'I told you to keep out of the mines,' he said.

Then he shut the door. Mary and Andy were left in the half light of the lamp, listening to Jack put the lock on the door. They heard him speaking to Martin.

'We'll leave the kids there for the moment,' he said. 'Then we'll come back this afternoon and pull down the roof of this tunnel. That way, when people realise the kids are missing and start to look for them, they won't look down here. No one will be able to get in. It'll just look like an old mine where the roof's fallen in.'

Andy hit the door a couple of times and heard Jack shout, 'No one can hear you.'

Realising that Jack was right, he stopped. He felt Mary's hand take hold of his arm.

'Andy!' Her voice sounded shaky. 'What are we going to do?'

He turned and looked at her. She wasn't crying, but she looked as if she might. She could be like that: fine until they really got into trouble, and then she stopped being fine and started crying. It wasn't the first time this had happened.

'I don't know what we're going to do,' he said, holding her hand in his. 'But at least we've got some light.'

He picked up the lamp and held it so that they could look at the door.

'That's quite a thick door,' he said, 'and the lock on the outside looked strong. I don't think we're going to be able to get out through there – which means we have to try the other way.'

'What? You mean go further into the mine?' asked Mary.
'Yes.'

Neither of them spoke for a moment, thinking about this.

Then Mary said, 'Actually that's not a bad idea. Dad told me there were so many mine tunnels that at one time you could go from Arkendale to Swaledale under ground.'

Andy said nothing for a moment.

Then he said, 'We're going to have to be very careful. I mean Dad wasn't joking when he said these mines were dangerous.'

'No, he wasn't,' agreed Mary. She was looking happier now they had decided what to do. 'Anyway, let's get started. We have to get out of here and tell Lord Fitch what's happening.'

Andy held up the lamp again and led the way further into the mine. The lamp gave out enough light to see a few metres ahead. Slowly, the teenagers walked deeper into the hillside. The roof of the tunnel was low and in places it was narrow, but they kept going. The tunnel seemed to be climbing, going uphill. In one wider part of the tunnel they passed an old metal truck left there for over a hundred years by lead miners of the past.

Then, after half an hour, they came to the stones. A lot of stones. Some were large, more like rocks. And they rose from the floor of the tunnel to the roof. There was no way through.

'The roof's fallen in,' said Andy quietly. 'There's no way through.'

'Oh no,' whispered Mary. Her voice sounded shaky again. 'We're stuck.'

Andy put the lamp on the ground. Then he picked up a large stone and gave it to Mary.

'Put that down behind you,' he said very quietly. 'Let's see how many stones and rocks there are here. But now we have to be really, really careful. The roof's fallen in once. We don't want it to happen again.'

Mary turned and put the stone down on the floor of the tunnel a few metres behind her. Andy picked up another stone and gave it to Mary. She did the same with that one. Together, slowly and carefully, without speaking, they started to take down the wall of stones and rocks in front of them and move it behind them.

Suddenly the stones moved a little, on their own. Andy and Mary immediately stopped, their hearts in their mouths. They didn't move for almost a minute; then Andy looked at Mary, nodded, and they started again.

Slowly but surely, the wall seemed to be coming down. Andy lifted the lamp and looked ahead. He smelled the air.

'There's fresh air up ahead,' he whispered. 'We must be close to a way out.'

He put the lamp down again and went back to picking up stones and passing them to his sister. After a few more minutes of this, he stopped again.

'I think we can get through there now,' he whispered. 'I'll go first and then turn round and light the way for you. Try not to touch the roof when you come through.'

Then he got down on his hands and knees and pulled himself along the tunnel to the other side of the stones. He turned and held up the light as Mary started to come through. She was almost through when there was a sudden noise above them. Again they both stopped moving. But Andy suddenly realised this wasn't the right thing to do. Quickly, he put the lamp down and reached back towards Mary with both hands. He took Mary's hands in his and pulled her as hard and fast as he could towards him. As he did so, there was another loud noise and dirt and stones and rocks started to fall from the roof of the tunnel. The lamp was knocked on its side and went out.

LOOKING BACK

 1 Check your answer to *Looking forward* on page 43.

ACTIVITIES

2 Complete the sentences with the names in the box.

| Jack (x2)   Jack and Martin   Martin   Mary   Poppy |

1 *Jack and Martin* go into the mine.

2 .... barks at the twins.

3 .... catches Mary.

4 .... catches Andy.

5 .... locks Andy and Mary in the room.

6 .... almost starts crying.

3 Are the sentences true (*T*) or false (*F*)?

1 Andy and Mary hide very near the mine. $\boxed{F}$

2 There is a dog in one of the Land Rovers. $\square$

3 Poppy catches a bird. $\square$

4 Poppy sees Andy and Mary before the men see them. $\square$

5 Andy and Martin are going to go back to the mine the next day. $\square$

6 The twins don't have a light in the tunnel. $\square$

7 In the tunnel, Andy can see the sky. $\square$

8 The roof of the tunnel starts to fall. $\square$

4 <u>Underline</u> the correct words in each sentence.

1 *Poppy* / *Jack* didn't go into the mine.
2 Jack and Martin left the mine with *one box* / *lots of boxes*.
3 *Mary* / *Mary's bike* fell to the ground.
4 Mary *can* / *can't* see gold in one of the boxes.
5 The tunnel *is* / *isn't* completely flat.
6 Andy and Mary move the wall of stones *in front of* / *behind* them.

5 Answer the questions.

1 Where do the teenagers leave their bikes?

2 Why can't the twins escape on their bikes?

3 Where are Jack and Martin going to take the boxes?

4 When will Jack and Martin come back to the mine?

LOOKING FORWARD

• •

6 Tick (✓) what you think happens in the next two chapters.

1 Andy and Mary escape. ☐
2 Someone tells Lord Fitch about Jack and Martin. ☐

Chapter 8

Getting out

Everything went quiet. Mary and Andy lay on the floor of the tunnel beside each other.

'Are you OK?' whispered Andy.

'I think so,' said Mary. Her voice sounded even shakier than before.

Andy reached out and found the lamp. He shook it and it lit up again.

He looked over at Mary. Then he looked back. Behind them, in the very place where Mary had been moments before, a new wall of rocks and stones had fallen from the roof.

Andy had pulled her through just in time. There was dirt all over her face. His was probably the same, he thought.

'Come on,' he said. 'Let's get out of here.'

He half stood up – the roof was very low here – and then helped Mary up.

He turned round with some difficulty and they started again, moving slowly along the mine. Five minutes later the tunnel turned a corner and they could see light.

'We've done it,' said Mary, excitedly.

'Not yet,' said Andy, looking along the tunnel. 'There are still a hundred metres or so to go. And we still need to be careful.'

Slowly, they made their way along the tunnel, putting their feet down carefully and trying not to touch the roof. As they got near to the light and the end of the tunnel, Andy realised there was still one more problem to take care of before they were free. The end of the tunnel did not come out on the side

of a hill. It went straight up for about ten metres into the open
air; the side walls were completely flat with no steps cut in
them, and over the top of this entrance to the mine were some
metal bars.

'Oh no,' said Mary when she saw it all. 'What are we going
to do now?'

Andy looked round him. There were a few stones on
the floor of the mine: some large, some small. He felt in his
pockets: money, pen, piece of chocolate. Nothing useful. He
took out the chocolate, broke it in half, gave one piece to Mary
and ate the other himself.

He looked at the hole that went straight up.

'It's not very wide, that hole,' he said. 'Give me a leg up.'

Mary put her hands together. Andy put one foot in her
hands and then stood up. Mary pushed upwards and Andy
got himself up into the hole. He had his back on one side and
his feet on the other. Pushing back with his hands and forward

with his feet, he moved his body up a little, then he moved his feet and hands up. He did the same thing again. Little by little, he moved up towards the metal bars at the top.

'Be careful, Andy,' said Mary from below.

As he got closer to the top, Andy could see there was a kind of door in the bars. He reached a hand up and pushed and pulled at it. It didn't open. He climbed further and put his head against the bars. He needed to see why it wouldn't open. There was a lock on the outside – an old one. Andy looked at it carefully, then he started to go back down towards Mary.

A metre or two from the bottom he stopped.

'Find me a stone that's about this size,' he said, opening his hand and showing her what he meant. 'And let me have your belt.'

Mary took off her belt and passed it up to him. He put it in one of his pockets. She looked round and found a stone that was about the right size. She threw that up too. He caught it and put it in the other pocket.

'What are you going to do?' she asked.

'There's a door through those bars up there,' he answered. 'If I can break the lock with this stone, then we can get out.'

'Why do you need the belt?' asked Mary.

'You'll see,' he replied.

Slowly, Andy made his way back up to the bars. When he got there, he put Mary's belt through his and then through the bars. Then he tied it round the bars. Now at least there was much less danger of falling to the bottom and killing himself. He took out the stone and reached through the bars. He hit the lock hard three times. Nothing. He tried again. Pieces of the stone flew off. He tried again. This time there was a different kind of noise. He looked at the lock. It had broken. He threw the stone out of the top of the mine, took off the lock and pushed open the door.

'Great! Well done, Andy!' He heard Mary's voice from below. Quickly, he untied her belt and put it back in his pocket. Then he worked his way back down towards the bottom. He moved down as far as he could.

'I'm going to have to pull you up,' he said. 'Come up through my legs and go up in front of me.'

He reached down and took Mary's hand. She was much lighter than him. He pulled her up. She got her arms through his legs and pushed herself upwards.

She got herself into the hole in the same way as Andy but a little bit above him. Together they moved up towards the open air. At the top Mary climbed out of the open door. Then she put a hand back to help her brother through. They both fell back on the grass looking at the hills round about, happy to be out in the fresh air, away from the dangers of the old mine.

Suddenly Mary sat up and looked at her watch.

'It's nearly eight o'clock,' she said. 'We have to get to Lord Fitch and tell him what's happening.'

She looked around at the hills. There were no houses anywhere and no roads.

'Where are we?' she asked.

They looked around. They couldn't see any part of the countryside that they knew. They looked all around again.

'That hill there,' said Mary, looking at one not too far away. 'That could be Mount Calva. We don't usually see it from this side but I think we've cycled near here before.'

Mount Calva is a hill, not really a mountain, and lies between Swaledale and Arkendale. Andy looked across at it.

'You could be right,' he said. 'Anyway, if we walk towards it, we should find a road fairly soon.'

They started walking across the hillside, Mount Calva in front of them. Soon they found a dirt road and began to follow that. The dirt road led down the side of a hill and after a few hundred metres joined a real road.

'I know where we are now,' said Andy. 'This is the road from Langthwaite to Surrender Bridge.'

They turned left and started walking.

'I don't expect many cars come along this road,' said Mary. 'We could have to walk the whole way back.'

But, at that moment, they heard a car behind them, though still some way away.

'We've got to stop this car and ask for a lift,' said Mary.

A small blue car came over the top of the hill and drove slowly down towards them.

Andy and Mary stood in the middle of the road, waving their hands for the driver to stop.

The car stopped a few metres away and the driver's door opened. A man got out. He had grey hair, a grey beard and a red face.

Chapter 9

Back to Arkle House

Andy and Mary looked at each other and were ready to turn and run, but the man pulled something out of his pocket and held it up.

'Don't run,' he said. 'I'm Dave Metcalfe, a private detective. I think you've got some information that could be very useful to me. I'd like to talk to you.'

Metcalfe walked slowly towards Andy and Mary. In his hand was an ID card with a photo of him. He showed it to the teenagers.

'I've been watching Arkle House for a few weeks now,' he explained. 'I'm working for the Goodwin family—'

'Then we've got to hurry.' Mary stopped Metcalfe talking. 'There's more gold than Lord Fitch knows about and some of his men are trying to steal it,' she said quickly.

'They said something about a helicopter,' said Andy. 'Maybe they're flying the gold out somewhere.'

Just then there was the noise of an engine away to the right behind Mount Calva. The three of them looked across as a helicopter flew round the side of the hill and started moving up Arkendale.

'Quick,' said Metcalfe. 'Into my car.'

They jumped into the car and drove off quickly towards Arkendale. On the way Andy and Mary told Metcalfe what they knew.

'If we don't stop them before they leave with the gold, we'll never catch them,' said Metcalfe. 'I want you to phone the police. It'll take them at least twenty minutes to get here from Richmond.'

'We'll have to use the payphone in Langthwaite,' said Mary. 'Mobiles don't work in this area.'

'I'll drop you near the payphone,' said Metcalfe. 'Then I'll try and stop the robbers before they take off.'

They drove over the top of the hill and down into Arkendale.

'Look,' said Andy. 'The helicopter's already landed and it's right in front of Arkle House.'

'And there are the Land Rovers,' said Mary as the two Land Rovers came round the side of the house and stopped near the helicopter.

Metcalfe stopped his car at the end of the road up to Arkle House. There was a phone box about a hundred metres away.

'Go and phone the police. Call this number.' Metcalfe gave Mary a piece of paper with a number on it. 'Ask for Inspector Rawlinson. He knows me. Tell him I told you to ring and that he should get out here with some police officers as soon as possible. He knows why I'm here.'

Andy and Mary jumped out of the car and ran to the phone box. Metcalfe drove off towards Arkle House.

Mary made the phone call and came out of the box.

'They're coming as soon as they can,' she said. 'Come on! We've got to go and help Mr Metcalfe.'

They started off towards the road to Arkle House, but then Mary stopped. 'Wait a minute,' she said. 'Let's go the other way.'

Andy looked at her questioningly.

'If we go this way, they'll see us coming,' she explained. 'If we go into Langthwaite and through the woods, we come out at the back of Arkle House. It might be better if they don't know we're coming.'

Andy knew she was right.

'Good idea,' he said. They raced through the village. It was still only half past eight in the morning and there was no one about. They ran up the hill to the woods. It took only a few minutes to run along the hillside through the trees and then they arrived at the back of Arkle House.

Quietly, they made their way down the hill and round to the side of the house. From their hiding place behind some small trees they could see the front of the house. Jack and Martin were taking the boxes of gold from the backs of the Land Rovers and putting them into the helicopter. There were only a few boxes left to move.

Just then two people came out of the front door of the house: Lord Fitch and Dave Metcalfe. Metcalfe's hands were tied behind his back and Lord Fitch was pushing him forwards.

There was a seat against the front of the house. Lord Fitch pushed Metcalfe down onto it.

'Stay there,' he ordered.

Andy heard Mary make a noise beside him.

'Lord Fitch,' whispered Mary. 'He must know about the gold. What's going on?'

Mary and Andy looked at each other. Suddenly everything fell into place.

'He's always known that there was lots of gold,' whispered Mary.

'And that it really belongs to the Goodwin family,' said Andy.

'So he said that there was only a little,' continued Mary, 'and—'

'Gave it to the Goodwin family so that it seemed that he was being really generous,' added Andy.

'But in fact he just wanted to keep as much as possible for himself,' finished Mary.

Andy and Mary continued to look at each other as they thought through what they had just discovered.

Then they looked out again towards the front of the house. Two boxes left.

Mary looked at her watch. The police wouldn't arrive for at least ten more minutes.

'We've got to stop him getting away,' she said.

They looked at each other, thinking hard. Then Andy spoke.

'I've got a plan,' he said. Then he asked, 'Do you know how to start a helicopter?'

LOOKING BACK

● ●

1 Check your answer to *Looking forward* on page 55.

ACTIVITIES

● ●

2 Are the sentences true (*T*) or false (*F*)?

1 Andy climbs up the hole very quickly. ☐ *F*
2 The lock at the top of the hole is new. ☐
3 Andy breaks the lock with a belt. ☐
4 At nearly eight o'clock, the teenagers are out of the hole. ☐
5 The man with the grey beard is a policeman. ☐
6 Andy and Mary get into Metcalfe's car. ☐

3 Match the two parts of the sentences.

1 The roof doesn't fall in on Mary because ☐ *c*
2 Andy and Mary don't stand up in the tunnel because ☐
3 The twins can't get out of the hole because ☐
4 Andy needs a stone ☐
5 Andy ties Mary's belt to the bars because ☐
6 Andy and Mary stop a car ☐

a to break the lock.
b they didn't want to touch the roof.
~~c~~ Andy pulls her away.
d to ask for help.
e there are some metal bars at the top of it.
f he doesn't want to fall.

66

4 Put the sentences in order.

1 A helicopter lands at Arkle House. ☐
2 Mary speaks to the police. ☐
3 Andy and Mary run to a phone box. ☐
4 Andy and Mary tell Metcalfe their story. ☐1☐
5 Metcalfe leaves Andy and Mary near Arkle House. ☐
6 Andy and Mary hide and watch Arkle House. ☐
7 The robbers stop their Land Rovers next to the helicopter. ☐
8 Andy and Mary understand what is happening. ☐

5 Answer the questions.

1 Who is Dave Metcalfe and why is he in the area?

....

2 What does Metcalfe ask Andy and Mary to do?

....

3 What happens to Metcalfe at Arkle House?

....

4 What do Andy and Mary learn about Lord Fitch?

....

LOOKING FORWARD
• •

6 Predict what happens in the final chapters.

1 What is Andy's plan?

....

2 Will the police arrest Lord Fitch?

....

Chapter 10

Stopping the helicopter

Mary looked at her brother in complete surprise.

'No,' she answered.

'I do,' said Andy. 'With a key.'

'But you can't fly,' said Mary.

'I know I can't,' replied Andy. 'But if there's a key in that helicopter and I can take it out, then they can't fly either.'

'Where's the pilot?' asked Mary.

'I don't know,' replied Andy. 'Maybe it's Lord Fitch himself.'

There was just one box left.

Andy looked at the helicopter and the ground around it. They couldn't get much closer than they already were.

'I'll get the key,' said Mary. 'I can run faster than you, Mr Slow.'

Andy looked at her. She had been a bit shaky down in the mine but now she was fine again. And she was right: she was faster than him. She didn't often let him forget it.

'I'll run out first and get them to come after me,' he said. 'How long will you need?'

'Enough time to get the key and then get away,' answered Mary. 'If I can get down the road as far as Arkle Beck, I can throw the key in the river. It'll take them more than ten minutes to find it in there.'

Jack and Martin picked the last box out of the Land Rover and put it in the helicopter. Then they walked over to Lord Fitch.

'I'm going now,' said Andy.

He came out from behind the trees, running as fast as he

could. At first he ran towards the three men.

'They need to think they can catch me,' he thought. 'Then they'll come after me so that Mary can get to the helicopter.'

As he ran, he shouted, 'Mr Metcalfe! Mr Metcalfe! Run! Run! You must run now!'

Andy saw Metcalfe stand up, his hands still tied. Jack and Martin's mouths fell open in surprise as Andy ran towards them. But then he turned away and started running down the road towards Langthwaite.

'Get that detective, Jack!' Fitch shouted as Metcalfe started to run away from the house. 'Come on, Martin. We'll get the boy.' And he started running down the road after Andy, with Martin behind him.

Andy knew the men would catch him before he reached the village. But that didn't matter. Mary just needed time to get the key from the helicopter.

Metcalfe had reached an open field and was running across it. Jack was running after him and getting closer.

Mary came out from behind the trees and ran to the helicopter. She opened the door and looked inside. There, right in front of the pilot's seat, was the key. She took it out of the lock, holding it in her hand, and got back out of the helicopter. She heard a shout. Martin, while chasing Andy, suddenly realised that he hadn't seen Mary. He had stopped to look round for her and had seen her get out of the helicopter. He was already running back.

Mary looked the other way.

Jack had caught Metcalfe and was bringing him back. She looked at Martin again. It would be difficult to reach the river before him. Perhaps it was a better idea to hide the key in the trees.

Mary raced into the trees. As soon as the men could no longer see her, she made a small hole in the ground at the bottom of a tree. She dropped the key into the hole and put some earth on top, then put leaves on top of that.

She heard Martin entering the woods.

Mary decided not to run. The noise would let Martin know where she was. She moved slowly and quietly away from the noise that Martin was making and hid behind some thick, low trees. Martin went past, running noisily and talking to himself. Mary moved back towards the house. She looked out from the place where she and Andy had hidden before. Metcalfe was back on the seat in front of the house, Jack watching him. Lord Fitch was bringing Andy back up from the Langthwaite Road, holding her brother's arm up behind his back. From where she was, Mary could also see the road to Reeth, far off, coming round the bottom of Mount Calva. She could also see three flashing blue lights. The police would not be long.

Lord Fitch and Andy reached the helicopter.

Martin returned.

'I can't find the girl anywhere,' he said. 'What do you want us to do?'

'She'll go back to where she's staying,' said Lord Fitch. 'Gladys Whitehead's house. Do you know it?'

'Yes,' replied Jack.

Lord Fitch pushed Andy towards Martin. 'Tie him up. And tie him and Metcalfe together. I don't want any more escapes.' He turned back towards Jack.

'Go down to the village. Get the girl before she gets to Gladys's or we're in real trouble.'

Mary looked out again. The police cars had started coming up the road towards Arkle House. No one had seen them yet.

'Are you looking for me?' said Mary, stepping out from behind the trees.

There was a moment of quiet as everyone looked at her. At that moment Lord Fitch realised that something was very wrong. He looked down from the house to the road and saw the police cars on their way up.

'Police,' he shouted.

Jack turned and ran. Lord Fitch pulled Andy back from Martin and reached into his pocket. A moment later he was holding a gun to Andy's head, his other arm round his neck. The three cars came to a stop, stones flying everywhere. Doors opened. Police officers ran out. Some chased after Jack. Martin had gone too. The rest of the officers stood and watched Lord Fitch.

'Stay back or the boy gets it,' he said.

Chapter 11

Catching the criminals

One of the police officers took a step forward. He was close to Lord Fitch but not close enough to reach him. Not while he had a gun at Andy's head.

'Don't move!' shouted Lord Fitch, pushing the gun hard against Andy's head.

The policeman spoke, 'Lord Fitch, I'm Inspector Rawlinson, North Yorkshire Police. It's all over.'

Lord Fitch took a step to the side, pulling Andy with him. Andy had both hands on the arm round his neck and looked afraid.

'It's not over,' said Lord Fitch. He moved again to the side, towards the helicopter. 'I can still get out of here.'

He continued to move until he was by the door to the helicopter.

'As soon as I've started the engines, you can have him – but keep away from the helicopter or I'll shoot,' he said.

At that moment he looked into the helicopter and saw that the key was missing.

'Where's the key?' he said angrily. 'Who's taken the key?'

He looked from one to the other at the people standing around him, his eyes finally coming to rest on Mary. His eyes were burning angrily. Mary could see the danger coming.

'You! You took it.' His voice was full of hate. 'You stupid girl!' Lord Fitch threw Andy to one side, put both hands on the gun and brought it round towards Mary.

Rawlinson knew this was the moment. He threw himself forward at Lord Fitch, arriving just as the gun fired. Mary had

seen what was going to happen and jumped to one side, falling behind a small tree.

As Rawlinson and Lord Fitch fell to the ground, two police officers ran towards them. It was all over in seconds. One officer took the gun; the other held Lord Fitch to the ground, pulled his hands behind his back and put on some handcuffs. A moment or two later other officers arrived back with Jack and Martin.

Mary stood up and came out from behind the tree. Andy ran over to her.

'I'm OK,' she said. 'I'm OK. What about you?'

'I'm OK,' he said. He took her hand.

Just then a black car drove up to the house and David Lawson got out. He was wearing a business suit and looked ready to start his day's work.

'What on earth's going on here?' he asked, looking at the police officers holding down Lord Fitch. Then he saw Andy and Mary as they ran towards him and threw their arms round him.

'Dad! Dad!' said Mary. 'There was more gold than we realised and Lord Fitch was trying to keep it all for himself.'

'And Martin and Jack were working for him. They were going to fly the gold out in the helicopter,' added Andy.

'Wait a minute! Wait a minute!' said David Lawson.

He turned to Inspector Rawlinson.

'What's going on?' he asked.

'Are you the father of these two?' asked Inspector Rawlinson, brushing dirt off his trousers.

'Yes,' answered David Lawson.

'I'm Inspector Rawlinson, North Yorkshire Police. Your children are brilliant. They've done very well. I'd like to thank them.'

'Why?' said David Lawson. 'What have they done?'

'Well, it was their phone call that brought us here and allowed us to catch these three.'

'Oh,' said David Lawson, a surprised look on his face. He looked questioningly first at Mary, then at Andy, but said nothing.

'In fact, Inspector,' said Metcalfe, who was still sitting on the seat in front of the house, 'you'll need to give them an even bigger thank you when you hear the complete story.'

One of the officers had untied Metcalfe but, even so, David Lawson gave him a strange look. He realised that this was the man Gladys had talked about the night before.

'What story?' asked David Lawson.

'It's all right, Dad,' said Mary, looking up at her father. 'We've just been doing a bit of detective work. At first we thought Jack and Martin were stealing gold from Lord Fitch.'

'But then we discovered Lord Fitch was stealing gold from the Goodwins,' continued Andy.

'I don't understand,' said David La wson.

'It's all right,' said Mary. 'We'll explain it all to you later.'

'You'll have lots of time to listen to it,' said Andy.

'What do you mean "I'll have lots of time"?' asked David Lawson.

'Well,' said Mary. 'I think the police are going to take Lord Fitch away and that means you're going to be out of a job.'

YORKSHIRE EVENING NEWS
Police thank twins for catching robbers
Six years in prison for the Arkendale Three

Inspector Rawlinson of the North Yorkshire Police said a special thank you today to two young teenagers for their help in catching the three robbers now known as the Arkendale Three.

'Andrew and Mary Lawson were a very great help to us,' he said. 'In fact, if it wasn't for these brave and intelligent teenagers, these three criminals might not be going to prison today.'

Lord Fitch, owner of Arkle House in Arkendale and two of his workers were each sent to prison for six years for trying to steal over £5 million worth of gold that belonged to the Goodwin family.

The gold was found in a disused lead mine near Arkle House. However, it was clear from papers found at Arkle House that the gold once belonged to Sir Francis Goodwin, owner of the house in the nineteenth century. Although Lord Fitch knew this, he was planning to fly the gold out of the country to his bank in Switzerland.

Twins, Andrew and Mary Lawson, realising that something strange was happening in Arkendale, decided to find out what was going on. During their search for the truth, they were locked in an old mine tunnel by Lord Fitch's men. However, the brave teenagers escaped and called the Richmond police in time to stop the robbers from leaving the country.

LOOKING BACK

● ●

1 Check your answer to *Looking forward* on page 67.

ACTIVITIES

● ●

2 Underline the correct words in each sentence.

1 Andy wants to steal the key from the *helicopter* / *Land Rover*.
2 Mary comes out from behind *the trees* / *a wall* and takes the key.
3 Mary hides the key in *the river* / *a hole in the ground*.
4 The robbers catch *Mary* / *Andy*.
5 There are *two* / *three* police cars in the distance.
6 *Lord Fitch* / *Martin* takes out his gun.

3 Complete the sentences with the names in the box.

> Jack   the Goodwin family   Martin
>
> Lord Fitch   Inspector Rawlinson
>
> ~~Detective Metcalfe~~   David Lawson

1 *Detective Metcalfe* couldn't use his hands.
2 .... runs after Detective Metcalfe.
3 .... and Lord Fitch run after Andy.
4 .... has got a gun.
5 .... saves Mary's life.
6 .... is going to lose his job.
7 The gold belonged to ....

4 Are the sentences true (*T*) or false (*F*)?

1 Andy and Mary plan to fly the helicopter. ☐ *F*
2 Jack and Martin put all the boxes into the helicopter. ☐
3 Mary doesn't run when she's in the woods. ☐
4 Lord Fitch tries to kill Andy. ☐
5 David didn't know that Metcalfe was a detective. ☐
6 Mary and Andy are going to explain everything to their father. ☐

5 <u>Underline</u> the correct words in each sentence.

1 The police thanked *David / Andrew and Mary* Lawson for helping them catch three criminals.
2 *David Metcalfe / Inspector Rawlinson* said that without the twins' help, the robbers could still be free.
3 The Arkendale Three are *Lord Fitch, Martin and Jack / David, Andrew and Mary Lawson*.
4 *Martin and Jack / The twins* were each sent to prison for six years.
5 The *North Yorkshire Police / robbers* were trying to steal over £5 million in gold.
6 *David Metcalfe / Lord Fitch* wanted to fly the gold to his bank in Switzerland.

6 Answer the questions.

1 Why doesn't Mary throw the key into the river?
....

2 What happens to Jack and Martin?
....

3 How does Mary avoid the gunfire?
....

4 Who catches Lord Fitch?
....

Glossary

[1]**lord** (page 6) *noun*   in the UK, a word used before the name of a man of very high social position

[2]**dale** (page 7) *noun*   in the north of England, the low area between mountains or hills

[3]**dig** (page 8) *verb*   to make a hole in the ground by moving some of the ground away

[4]**binoculars** (page 11) *noun*   two tubes with glass at the ends that you look through to see things that are far away

[5]**scone** (page 18) *noun*   a small kind of bread/cake that people eat in the afternoon with a cup of tea. Scones are often eaten with jam and thick cream.

[6]**gate** (page 24) *noun*   a door in a fence or outside wall

[7]**why on earth** (page 35) *expression*   used when you are extremely confused, surprised or angry about something

[8]**brain** (page 38) *noun*   the part inside your head that controls thoughts, memory, feelings and activities

[9]**dry stone wall** (page 44) *noun*   a type of wall often found in the north of England. The wall is made only of stones. Nothing is used to hold the stones together.

[10]**tunnel** (page 49) *noun*   a long passage under the ground or through a mountain